Podcasting Success Blueprint

The Complete Guide to Launching, Growing, and Monetizing Your Podcast: Proven Strategies for Beginners and Pros

Alex Reid

Alex Reid

Disclaimer
This book is intended to provide helpful and informative material on the subjects addressed. It is not a substitute for professional advice. The author and publisher make no representations or warranties regarding the accuracy, applicability, or completeness of the content of this book. The author and publisher disclaim any liability, loss, or risk, directly or indirectly, that may arise from the use or application of the contents of this book.

First Edition
Printed in the United States of America

Alex Reid

Introduction

Imagine this: you have a passion you can't stop talking about, an idea that feels bigger than you, or a skill that you know could change people's lives. But how do you share it with the world? This was the same question I faced years ago when I first ventured into the world of sound and audio entertainment. With years of experience in podcasting, speaking, and creating engaging audio content, I've witnessed firsthand how powerful a podcast can be—not only as a platform for sharing knowledge but also as a tool for building meaningful connections.

Whether you want to inspire, educate, or entertain, podcasting offers you a chance to amplify your voice. But starting a podcast can feel overwhelming. Between figuring out equipment, learning how to structure episodes, and finding an audience, it's easy to feel lost before you even record your first word. That's exactly why I created this book.

Who This Book is For

This guide is for anyone who's ever felt a spark to share their message through podcasting. Maybe you're a complete beginner with no technical background, or perhaps you've dabbled in audio but want to take things to the next level. If you're an entrepreneur, educator, or creative with a story or skill that could benefit others, this book will take you step-by-step through the process of launching and growing a podcast.

How to Use This Book

This book is designed to be your go-to roadmap, guiding you from idea to launch and beyond. In each chapter, you'll find actionable tips, simple explanations, and best practices, all drawn from years of experience and industry insight. You'll get a complete picture of what it takes to start a podcast and maintain it successfully, whether you're doing it as a hobby or with professional aspirations.

Feel free to skip around based on your needs. Maybe you want to start by getting your equipment set up, or perhaps you need help structuring your content. Each chapter is crafted to stand alone as a helpful resource while still building toward the bigger picture of creating a podcast that resonates.

By the end of this book, you'll have the tools, confidence, and insider knowledge to start a podcast that stands out. Whether it's sharing your expertise, amplifying your brand, or creating a community, I'm excited to join you on this journey and help you turn your podcasting dreams into a reality.

Let's dive in and start crafting a podcast that's as unique as your voice.

Table of Contents

Alex Reid

Alex Reid

Chapter 1

Getting Started with Podcasting

Why Podcasting?

Podcasting has become one of the most captivating and accessible forms of media today. It offers a unique blend of intimacy and reach, allowing creators to speak directly to their listeners—whether they're commuting to work, doing household chores, or unwinding at the end of the day. Unlike video or written content, which demands full attention, podcasts create an immersive, hands-free experience, making them an ideal companion for the multitaskers of our fast-paced world.

Imagine having a platform where you can discuss the topics you're passionate about, connect with like-minded individuals, and even build a community around your ideas. This is the magic of podcasting. It's a powerful medium for sharing expertise, engaging in meaningful conversations, and telling stories that resonate on a personal level. Whether you want to entertain, educate, or simply share your thoughts, podcasting is a place where your voice can make an impact.

Podcasting also offers freedom. You can shape your show however you like—no network executives or complex production teams are needed to approve your content. All you need is a good idea, a bit of equipment, and the will to get started. It's a creative playground where you control the narrative, the tone, and the direction.

For readers considering starting a podcast, this journey is about more than just producing episodes; it's about building something that listeners come to anticipate and love. Podcasts have the power to inspire, inform, and connect. By starting your own podcast, you're not only expressing yourself but also inviting others to be part of your story. Whether you're sharing personal experiences, interviewing experts, or creating fictional worlds, podcasting provides a platform that's truly yours.

So, if you've ever wanted to share your voice with the world, now is the perfect time to start.

Key Requirements for Success

Starting a podcast is an exciting journey, but to create a show that truly resonates with listeners, it's important to understand the foundational requirements for success. Let's break down the essential skills, time commitments, and initial resources you'll need, and see how each one contributes to producing a high-quality podcast.

Essential Skills

1. Communication Skills

At the heart of any great podcast is effective communication.

- **Clarity and Articulation**: Being able to express your thoughts clearly helps listeners understand and stay engaged with your content.

- **Storytelling Ability**: Crafting compelling narratives keeps your audience hooked from start to finish.

- **Active Listening** (for interview podcasts): If you're hosting guests, listening attentively allows you to ask insightful follow-up questions.

How it contributes: Strong communication makes your content accessible and enjoyable, encouraging listeners to return for more episodes.

2. Technical Skills

You don't need to be an audio engineer, but some basic technical know-how is important.

- **Recording Techniques**: Understanding how to use your microphone and recording software ensures clear audio.

- **Editing Skills**: Knowing how to edit out mistakes and enhance sound quality improves the listener's experience.

- **Troubleshooting**: Being able to solve minor technical issues keeps your production process smooth.

How it contributes: Technical proficiency ensures your podcast sounds professional, which can significantly impact listener retention and credibility.

3. Organizational Skills

Good organization keeps your podcast consistent and sustainable.

- **Content Planning**: Outlining episodes in advance helps maintain a coherent theme and schedule.

- **Time Management**: Allocating time for each stage—research, recording, editing—ensures you meet your release deadlines.

- **Project Management**: Keeping track of tasks, especially if you're collaborating with others, keeps everything on track.

How it contributes: Organization leads to consistency, a key factor in building and retaining an audience over time.

Time Commitment

Launching and maintaining a podcast does require a dedicated investment of time.

1. Preparation Time

- **Researching Topics**: Delving into your subject matter adds depth to your episodes.

- **Scripting/Outlining**: Preparing what you'll say helps prevent rambling and keeps episodes focused.

How it contributes: Thorough preparation results in informative and engaging content that provides value to your listeners.

2. Recording Time

- **Actual Recording**: Depending on your format, recording can take as long as the episode itself or longer if retakes are needed.

How it contributes: Allocating sufficient time ensures you're not rushed, leading to a more relaxed and natural delivery.

3. Editing Time

- **Post-Production**: Editing can take double or triple the length of the raw recording.

How it contributes: Careful editing removes distractions like pauses and filler words, enhancing the overall quality.

4. Promotion Time

- **Marketing Efforts**: Engaging with your audience on social media, responding to comments, and promoting upcoming episodes.

How it contributes: Effective promotion grows your listener base and fosters a community around your podcast.

Initial Resources

Starting a podcast doesn't have to break the bank, but some initial investments are necessary.

1. Equipment

- **Microphone**: A good-quality microphone is crucial for clear sound.

- **Headphones**: Over-ear headphones help you monitor audio levels and detect issues.

- **Pop Filter**: This accessory reduces plosive sounds (like hard "p" and "b" noises).

How it contributes: Quality equipment elevates the sound of your podcast, making it more pleasant for listeners.

2. Recording Software

- **Digital Audio Workstation (DAW)**: Software like Audacity (free) or Adobe Audition (paid) for recording and editing.

How it contributes: Reliable software allows you to record and fine-tune your episodes effectively.

3. Recording Space

- **Quiet Environment**: A room with minimal background noise and echo.

How it contributes: A suitable recording space reduces unwanted sounds, improving audio quality without extensive editing.

4. Hosting Service

- **Podcast Hosting Platform**: Services like Anchor or Libsyn store your audio files and distribute your podcast to platforms like Apple Podcasts and Spotify.

How it contributes: A good hosting service ensures your podcast is easily accessible to listeners worldwide.

By focusing on developing these skills, dedicating the necessary time, and investing in the right resources, you're setting a solid foundation for your podcast's success. Each component plays a vital role in creating a show that's not only high in quality but also engaging and sustainable in the long run.

Remember, every successful podcaster started where you are now—with an idea and the willingness to learn. As you grow and gain experience, these elements will become second nature, allowing you to focus more on delivering great content and connecting with your audience.

Understanding the Podcasting Landscape

Podcasting has evolved into a dynamic industry, captivating millions of listeners worldwide. Its growth has been explosive in recent years, with new shows emerging daily across various genres. Popular genres include true crime, comedy, news, self-improvement, and educational content, each catering to distinct audiences with unique interests. While true crime draws listeners through suspenseful storytelling, comedy podcasts often attract younger listeners looking for entertainment. Educational podcasts, on the other hand, appeal to those seeking knowledge, whether it's learning about history, personal finance, or wellness. This diversity of genres means that there's space for almost every kind of interest and topic.

The podcasting audience is as diverse as its content. While listeners span all ages, demographics show that younger audiences—especially millennials and Gen Z—are the most avid consumers. According to recent studies, these age groups are particularly drawn to podcasts for their convenience and the ability to listen while multitasking. Additionally, many listeners enjoy the intimacy of podcasts, which often feature conversational tones and immersive storytelling. For new podcasters, understanding their potential audience's demographics and listening habits is key. It allows them to create content that resonates, keeping listeners engaged and eager for the next episode.

Successful podcasts often share some common traits that set them apart. For instance, *The Daily* by The New York Times has excelled in the news genre by providing listeners with concise, in-depth analysis of current events, delivered in a storytelling format. Similarly, *How I Built This* by Guy Raz has become a standout by interviewing entrepreneurs, providing unique insights into the journey of building successful companies. These shows succeed because they cater to their audience's curiosity while delivering consistent, high-quality content. They focus on their niche, use compelling narratives, and maintain a level of professionalism that draws listeners back again and again.

In my experience helping others launch their podcasts, I've seen firsthand how focusing on these core elements—targeting a specific audience, consistency, and quality—makes a tremendous difference. Many aspiring podcasters I've worked with start with enthusiasm but quickly realize the importance of developing a solid structure and understanding their audience's preferences. One podcaster I mentored, for example, turned her wellness podcast into a success by honing in on her audience's specific needs for practical, actionable advice. With a consistent release schedule, clear topic focus, and genuine engagement with listeners, she grew her podcast steadily, proving that with the right approach, any podcast can find its unique place in this ever-growing industry.

Chapter 2

Choosing Your Niche and Audience

Defining Your Podcast's Focus

One of the most exciting steps in starting a podcast is choosing a unique focus or niche. Finding a topic that resonates with both you and your potential listeners can set your show apart in a crowded market. To begin, think about areas you're genuinely passionate about or knowledgeable in. Passion and expertise help keep you motivated and ensure that your content remains fresh and engaging for the long haul.

Start by making a list of topics that spark your interest. These could be hobbies, personal interests, professional skills, or areas where you have unique insights. For example, if you're fascinated by history, your podcast could focus on historical mysteries or untold stories. If you're a personal finance enthusiast, you might consider a podcast on budgeting tips or financial independence. Don't limit yourself—write down everything that comes to mind, no matter how broad it seems at first. Once you have a list, try narrowing it down by asking yourself: Which topics can I talk about enthusiastically? Which would I be excited to research and discuss week after week?

Once you've identified a few potential topics, it's time to refine them into a focused niche. Consider combining two interests to create a unique angle. For instance, instead of a general podcast about wellness, you could focus on "wellness for working parents" or "wellness hacks for entrepreneurs." By targeting a specific group, you'll have a clearer focus and a better chance of connecting with a dedicated audience. A niche allows you to speak directly to the interests and needs of a particular group, increasing the likelihood that they'll return for every episode.

Another helpful exercise is to consider the "three C's": clarity, consistency, and commitment. Ask yourself if your topic is clear (will listeners instantly understand what your podcast is about?), consistent (can you produce regular content around this focus?), and something you can commit to long-term. These questions help refine your ideas, turning a broad interest into a clear, manageable niche that will serve as the foundation for a successful podcast.

Finding Your Target Audience

Identifying your target audience is crucial to building a podcast that resonates and grows over time. Understanding who you're creating content for helps you tailor episodes to their interests, preferences, and needs. Here are practical steps to help you identify and get to know your audience in a way that shapes every aspect of your podcast.

1. Define Your Ideal Listener

Begin by picturing your ideal listener. Ask yourself: Who would find my content valuable or entertaining? Consider factors like age, profession, interests, and lifestyle. For example, if you're starting a podcast on budgeting tips, your target audience might include young professionals, students, or parents who want to manage finances better. Write a profile of this ideal listener, noting their possible motivations for listening, their goals, and their challenges. This profile will serve as a helpful guide in keeping your content relevant to the people you want to reach.

2. Research Audience Interests and Pain Points

Once you've defined your ideal listener, dig deeper into what they care about. Research where they spend time online: look at forums, social media groups, and blogs that cover similar topics. Pay attention to the questions they're asking and the topics they discuss frequently. For example, if your podcast is about fitness for beginners, look at online communities where people ask about starting workouts, overcoming obstacles, and balancing fitness with busy lives. These are the types of questions you can answer in your podcast, creating valuable content that addresses specific pain points.

3. Study Listening Habits and Preferences

Understanding your target audience's listening habits will help you shape the length, style, and format of your episodes. Research shows that different audiences have varied preferences; some prefer short, 10–15 minute episodes they can consume quickly, while others enjoy longer, in-depth discussions. If you're targeting busy professionals, shorter, actionable episodes might work well. For audiences with more time, like stay-at-home parents or hobbyists, longer episodes may be appropriate. You can gain insights into these preferences by surveying potential listeners or observing popular podcasts in your niche.

4. Test and Gather Feedback

If possible, start by releasing a few sample episodes to gauge audience response. Encourage listeners to share their thoughts through reviews, emails, or social media. Pay close attention to the feedback you receive—listeners may suggest topics they'd love to hear more about, highlight parts they enjoyed, or even provide constructive criticism. This feedback loop allows you to continually refine your content, making it more aligned with your audience's needs and interests over time.

Researching Competitors

Researching competitors in your niche is essential for understanding what's already out there and identifying ways to make your podcast stand out. By analyzing similar shows, you can find both inspiration and potential gaps that represent opportunities to offer something unique. Here's a step-by-step approach to researching competitor podcasts effectively.

1. Identify Key Competitors

Start by searching for podcasts in your chosen niche on popular platforms like Apple Podcasts, Spotify, and Google Podcasts. Use keywords related to your topic, such as "wellness for entrepreneurs" or "personal finance tips." Note down the top shows, especially those with high ratings and large followings. Make a list of at least 5–10 podcasts to examine more closely. This list will give you a clearer picture of the landscape and help you understand what draws listeners in your niche.

2. Analyze Their Content and Structure

Listen to a few episodes of each competitor podcast and pay attention to their content and format. Look at the topics they cover, episode length, release frequency, and structure (such as whether it's interview-based, solo, or storytelling-focused).

Notice any patterns that indicate what's working well. For example, if you're interested in launching a self-improvement podcast, you may find that popular shows often feature expert guests or include actionable "takeaways" at the end of each episode. Understanding these details can help you see what appeals to the audience and what you may want to replicate or improve upon.

3. Evaluate Audience Engagement

Audience engagement is a strong indicator of a podcast's success. Check reviews and ratings to see what listeners appreciate or criticize. Read comments to discover common themes or features that resonate with the audience. For instance, do listeners love a particular host's storytelling approach or a guest's insights? Additionally, observe how competitors engage with their audience outside of the podcast—do they have active social media accounts, a website, or a newsletter? Engaging with listeners beyond the podcast can help build a community, and seeing what works for others can provide ideas for your own engagement strategies.

4. Identify Gaps and Opportunities

Finally, consider what's missing or underserved in competitor podcasts. Are there topics within the niche that aren't being covered in depth? Are there questions or issues mentioned in the reviews that you could address? For example, if you notice that personal finance podcasts rarely cover finance for freelancers, you could position your podcast to fill this gap. You might also notice an opportunity to change the tone— perhaps many podcasts in the niche are highly formal, and a more casual, approachable style could attract listeners. Finding these gaps gives you the chance to carve out your unique angle, allowing you to provide fresh value to the audience.

By researching competitors thoughtfully, you'll gain a better understanding of your niche and uncover opportunities to differentiate your podcast. This research lays the foundation for creating content that stands out, appeals to listeners, and provides a unique take on a familiar subject.

Chapter 3

Planning Your Content

Generating Fresh Episode Ideas and Themes

Planning your podcast content is like mapping out an adventure. You'll want a good mix of exciting one-time episodes and overarching themes that tie everything together. Here's a fresh approach to brainstorm ideas and keep your podcast lineup dynamic, relevant, and true to your audience.

---

1. Dive into Your Audience's World

First, go where your listeners hang out—social media groups, forums, industry blogs, and even competing podcasts' comment sections. Note the questions people are asking, the frustrations they express, and the trends they're buzzing about. This is your treasure trove of inspiration. Each common question or problem can be turned into an episode that directly addresses something your audience cares about. Think of it as a way to keep your finger on the pulse of what's meaningful to your listeners.

2. Create Mini-Series or Thematic Seasons

Breaking down big topics into a series of episodes (or even a season) is a fantastic way to keep listeners hooked. Let's say your podcast is about eco-friendly living; you could have a mini-series called "Green at Home," with each episode covering a different room in the house—kitchen, bathroom, laundry, etc. This episodic format not only gives structure but also adds depth. Listeners will appreciate the continuity and the chance to dive deep into a theme over multiple episodes.

3. Tap into Your Personal Experiences and Stories

Sometimes, the best ideas come from your own experiences or expertise. Share your stories, the challenges you've overcome, or the "aha" moments that changed your perspective. These personal episodes help your audience connect with you on a deeper level, and they bring authenticity to your content. If you're hosting a podcast on business, recounting lessons learned from your early days as an entrepreneur can be inspiring and relatable.

4. Invite Audience Participation

Involve your listeners directly by running Q&A episodes, polls, or topic requests. Post a question on social media, asking what they'd love to hear more about, or let them vote on the next episode topic. You could even take a unique approach by dedicating an episode to listener stories or feedback on past episodes. This not only gives you ready-made content but also builds community and loyalty as your audience feels more engaged with the show.

5. Follow Industry Trends and Seasonal Events

Stay current by keeping an eye on trends within your niche. If there's a big event, news story, or change in your field, cover it as soon as possible. These "hot topic" episodes are a great way to attract listeners searching for up-to-date information. Additionally, consider creating episodes around seasonal themes. For example, a finance podcast might feature episodes on budgeting for the holidays or filing taxes in the spring.

6. Mix Up Formats for Variety

Trying different formats keeps things exciting. Alternate between solo episodes, guest interviews, panel discussions, or even live Q&As. Variety in structure can inspire new angles for familiar topics and introduce new voices and perspectives, which keeps the podcast feeling fresh and engaging.

Keeping episode ideas flowing is all about being open to inspiration, listening to your audience, and finding new ways to engage with familiar themes. A well-planned content calendar that includes a mix of evergreen episodes, current topics, and thematic series will make sure your podcast always feels fresh, relevant, and valuable to your listeners.

Structuring Episodes for Maximum Engagement

Creating an engaging podcast episode is like crafting a great story—you need a beginning that hooks listeners, a middle that keeps them captivated, and an end that leaves them wanting more. The way you structure each episode impacts not only how your message is delivered but also how your listeners experience it. Here's how to organize your episodes to maximize engagement, plus a few lessons learned along the way.

1. Start Strong with a Hook

Every good episode starts with a great intro. You have about 10-15 seconds to grab your audience's attention, so make it count. Begin with a quick, catchy teaser of what's coming up: "Today, we're diving into the secrets behind productivity—and I'm sharing the one technique that changed my life!"

From my own experience, I've found that a relatable personal story or a surprising fact works wonders. For instance, I once opened an episode by sharing a quirky mishap from my early podcasting days—recording an entire interview, only to find out later that the mic wasn't plugged in! That little story set a lighthearted tone and built a connection with listeners right away.

2. Lay Out the Episode Roadmap

After hooking your listeners, it's a good idea to give a quick overview of what to expect. Think of this as the episode's roadmap. Tell your audience how you'll break down the topic and what key points you'll cover. Not only does this help set clear expectations, but it also builds anticipation. For example, in a podcast about productivity, you might say, "Today, we're going to cover three practical strategies, starting with the power of focus, then moving to time-blocking, and finally, ending with tips on avoiding burnout."

3. Dive into the Main Content with Engaging Transitions

Once you're into the main content, make sure it flows smoothly from one point to the next. Transitions are your best friend here; they keep listeners engaged and help prevent your content from feeling choppy. If you're moving from one tip to another, use phrases like, "Next up..." or, "On that note, let's talk about..." These subtle cues guide listeners effortlessly through your ideas.

One trick I picked up over time is to use relatable anecdotes between points. For example, in a podcast about business, you might transition from discussing strategy to talking about work-life balance by sharing a quick story about a time you stayed up late working and missed a family event. Listeners appreciate these real-life moments—they add depth to your points and keep the conversation natural.

4. End with a Strong Call to Action

Your call to action (CTA) is how you wrap things up and encourage your listeners to take the next step. This might be as simple as asking them to subscribe, rate, or share the episode if they enjoyed it. You can also direct them to your social media, website, or specific resources. For instance, "If you found these tips helpful, make sure to subscribe for more episodes, and follow us on Instagram for daily inspiration!"

In my early days of podcasting, I realized that the more specific the CTA, the better the response. For example, instead of saying, "Check out our website," try something more direct like, "Head over to our website to download the free productivity checklist that complements today's episode."

The secret to a well-structured episode lies in planning each segment thoughtfully—hooking them in the intro, guiding them through the main content with smooth transitions, and ending with a clear, compelling CTA. Each part plays a role in keeping listeners engaged and making them feel connected. And as I learned early on, adding a few personal touches or stories along the way transforms a structured outline into a memorable experience for your audience.

So, next time you sit down to plan an episode, remember: the structure isn't just about organization; it's about creating a journey that keeps listeners with you from start to finish.

Outlining and Scripting Your Podcast Episodes

Crafting an effective outline or script is essential for delivering clear and engaging content. Whether you prefer a loose outline or a detailed script, having a plan in place can keep your episodes focused and professional. Here's a step-by-step approach to outlining and scripting, with tips on finding the right level of detail for your style.

Step 1: Start with a Loose Outline

A loose outline is a high-level structure for your episode. Think of it as the episode's backbone. For example, let's say you're creating a podcast on productivity. Your outline might look like this:

1. **Introduction and Hook**

    o   Briefly share a surprising fact or personal story about productivity.

2. **Main Points**

    o   Point 1: Discuss the importance of focus and eliminating distractions.

    o   Point 2: Introduce time-blocking and its benefits.

    o   Point 3: Share tips on avoiding burnout.

3. **Conclusion and Call to Action**

    o   Summarize key points and encourage listeners to try one new productivity tip.

A loose outline gives you a sense of direction without being too rigid, allowing you to improvise and keep the conversation natural. This is ideal for hosts who enjoy a conversational, unscripted feel in their episodes. It also works well for co-hosted shows, where hosts can play off each other's points.

Step 2: Create a Detailed Outline for Specific Talking Points

If you prefer more structure but don't want to write out a full script, a detailed outline might be the right fit. In this approach, you expand on each point with sub-bullets, providing key phrases, examples, or questions. Here's an example of a detailed outline for the productivity episode:

1. **Introduction and Hook**
   o "Did you know that multitasking can reduce productivity by up to 40%?"
   o Brief story about a time you struggled with focus.

2. **Main Points**
   o **Point 1: Focus and Eliminating Distractions**
      ▪ Discuss how multitasking divides attention.
      ▪ Mention techniques like "batching similar tasks."
   o **Point 2: Time-Blocking**
      ▪ Define time-blocking and why it's effective.
      ▪ Personal anecdote about using time-blocking during a busy week.
   o **Point 3: Avoiding Burnout**
      ▪ Describe signs of burnout.
      ▪ Tips for creating balance and taking breaks.

3. **Conclusion and Call to Action**

> o "Pick one of these strategies to try this week and let us know how it goes!"

With a detailed outline, you have key points and transitions mapped out, which reduces the risk of forgetting details while still allowing for a conversational tone.

Step 3: Write a Full Script for Precision

For some episodes, especially if they involve technical content, storytelling, or specific language, a full script can be very useful. A word-for-word script gives you complete control over what you say, which is beneficial if you need to convey complex ideas clearly or if you're covering sensitive topics where wording matters. Here's an example of how a scripted section might look:

Introduction: "Welcome to [Podcast Name]! Today, we're diving into productivity secrets that could transform your workday. Did you know that multitasking can actually decrease productivity by up to 40%? I remember a time when I thought multitasking was the answer—until I realized I was actually getting less done."

Main Points - Point 1: "Our first tip is all about focus. When we try to do multiple things at once, we're actually reducing the quality of our work on each task. A great technique to stay focused is batching similar tasks. For example, if you have several emails to write, set aside time to handle them all at once, instead of switching back and forth throughout the day."

Writing a full script requires more preparation but ensures that you deliver each point precisely. It's ideal if you're aiming for a polished, highly-produced episode or if you're working on a solo show where you need to carry the entire narrative.

Step 4: Decide on the Right Approach for Each Episode

The level of scripting you choose can vary based on the episode's content and your comfort level. Here's a quick guide:

- **Loose Outline**: Ideal for casual, conversational episodes or co-hosted shows. It allows flexibility and spontaneity.

- **Detailed Outline**: Great for episodes that need structure without strict scripting, helping keep your points on track while allowing for a natural flow.

- **Full Script**: Best for technical topics, storytelling, or solo episodes where you need precision in language.

Outlining and scripting is all about finding the balance that works for you. Some podcasters stick to one approach, while others switch between styles depending on the episode. Experiment and discover what helps you deliver engaging, clear, and consistent content each time.

Chapter 4

Equipment and Software Essentials

Audio Equipment Basics

The quality of your podcast audio can make or break your listeners' experience, so investing in some essential equipment is a smart move. Fortunately, you don't have to spend a fortune—there are options to suit every budget. Here's a rundown of the basic equipment you'll need, from affordable options to higher-end choices, and how each piece contributes to your sound quality.

1. Microphone

A good microphone is the heart of any podcasting setup. The quality of your microphone will directly impact the clarity and warmth of your voice, helping you sound professional and polished. There are a few main types to consider:

- **USB Microphones**: Ideal for beginners, USB mics plug directly into your computer. They're affordable and easy to set up. The **Audio-Technica ATR2100x-USB** and **Blue Yeti** are popular choices in this category, offering quality sound for a reasonable price (typically around $70–$130).

- **XLR Microphones**: If you're aiming for studio-level audio, an XLR microphone is a great choice. These require an audio interface or mixer to connect to your computer, so they're a bit more complex. The **Shure SM7B** and **Rode PodMic** are top-tier options known for their rich, professional sound, though they come at a higher price point (around $100–$400).

How it impacts audio quality: A good microphone will capture the full range of your voice, minimize background noise, and give your audio a professional edge. USB mics are a great start, but upgrading to an XLR mic can make a noticeable difference if you're serious about podcasting.

2. Headphones

Wearing headphones while recording is essential for monitoring your sound. They allow you to hear exactly what your listeners will hear, helping you catch issues like background noise, mic pops, or volume imbalances as you record.

- **Closed-Back Headphones**: These are best for podcasting because they block out external noise and prevent audio "bleed" (when the sound from your headphones is picked up by the mic). The **Audio-Technica ATH-M50x** and **Sony MDR-7506** are both popular options in the $80–$150 range.

- **Budget-Friendly Headphones**: If you're on a tight budget, look for closed-back headphones like the **OneOdio Studio Pro-10** ($30–$50) that offer decent sound quality without breaking the bank.

How it impacts audio quality: Good headphones allow you to monitor your sound in real time, helping you catch mistakes before they end up in your final recording. This saves you time in editing and improves the overall quality of your podcast.

3. Pop Filter

A pop filter is a simple but effective tool that reduces "plosive" sounds—those hard "p" and "b" sounds that can cause unwanted audio spikes. It's a mesh screen that sits between you and the microphone, softening these sounds to keep your audio smooth and pleasant.

- **Basic Pop Filters**: Affordable options, like the **Aokeo Professional Pop Filter** or **Dragonpad Pop Filter**, cost around $10–$20 and do the job well.

- **Integrated Pop Filters**: Some microphones, like the Shure SM7B, have built-in pop filters, reducing the need for an external one.

How it impacts audio quality: A pop filter keeps your recordings free of harsh, distracting sounds, giving your podcast a polished feel. It's a small investment that makes a big difference, especially if you're close to the mic.

4. Boom Arm or Mic Stand

A boom arm or mic stand holds your microphone at the ideal height and distance, allowing you to stay comfortable and consistent in your recording position. It also helps reduce vibrations and accidental noise, especially if you tend to move around while speaking.

- **Affordable Boom Arms**: Options like the **Neewer Adjustable Boom Arm** and **InnoGear Boom Arm** (both around $15–$30) are good starter choices.

- **Higher-End Options**: If you want something more durable and stable, the **Rode PSA1** is a popular choice at around $100.

How it impacts audio quality: A boom arm or stand keeps your microphone steady and at a consistent angle, preventing fluctuations in sound quality due to movement.

5. Audio Interface or Mixer (for XLR Mics)

If you decide to use an XLR microphone, you'll need an audio interface or mixer to connect it to your computer. These devices amplify your mic's signal and allow you to control audio levels.

- **Entry-Level Interfaces**: The **Focusrite Scarlett 2i2** and **Behringer UMC22** (around $50–$150) are reliable options for beginners.

- **Mixers with More Control**: If you want advanced control over multiple audio sources, the **Rodecaster Pro** is a podcasting-focused mixer with premium features, though it's on the higher end (around $600).

How it impacts audio quality: An audio interface or mixer enhances the sound quality of your recordings, giving you more control over audio levels and enabling a cleaner, richer sound.

These pieces of equipment form the foundation of a quality podcasting setup. Starting with a USB mic, basic headphones, and a pop filter is a great way to begin without spending too much. As your podcast grows, you can invest in higher-end gear to further enhance your sound quality.

Recording Software Overview

Choosing the right recording software is key to producing a high-quality podcast. The software you use should fit your needs, whether you're looking for simplicity, advanced editing options, or special features. Here's a breakdown of some of the most popular recording software for podcasters: Audacity, GarageBand, and Adobe Audition.

---

1. Audacity

Overview: Audacity is a free, open-source audio editing software available on Windows, macOS, and Linux. It's beginner-friendly and provides all the essential tools you need to record, edit, and enhance your podcast audio.

- **Pros**:
  - Free to use, with no cost to access advanced features.
  - User-friendly interface that's ideal for beginners.
  - Offers a range of editing tools, such as cutting, trimming, noise reduction, and effects like equalization and reverb.
- **Cons**:
  - Lacks some advanced features found in paid software.
  - Limited to stereo or mono recording (no multitrack support for layering different audio sources).
  - Interface can look outdated to some users.
- **Special Features**: Audacity has powerful noise reduction tools, which are great for podcasters working in non-soundproofed spaces. It also allows for third-party plug-ins, making it highly customizable.

Best for: Beginners or those on a budget who need solid editing tools without a high learning curve.

Alex Reid

2. GarageBand

Overview: GarageBand is a free audio workstation developed by Apple, available on macOS and iOS. Known for its simple, intuitive design, it's often the first choice for Mac users who want an easy way to record and edit audio.

- **Pros**:
  - Free and pre-installed on most Apple devices, making it easily accessible.
  - Multitrack recording, which is useful for layering different audio sources.
  - Includes a variety of built-in sound effects, music loops, and audio filters.

- **Cons**:
  - Limited compatibility, as it's only available for Apple users.
  - May lack some of the detailed control found in professional audio software.
  - Limited export options for certain audio formats.

- **Special Features**: GarageBand is known for its easy-to-use interface and built-in music and sound effects. Its multitrack recording capabilities allow you to layer multiple audio tracks, making it ideal for podcasts that feature background music, sound effects, or multiple speakers.

Best for: Mac users who want a straightforward tool for recording and editing, especially for podcasts with music or multitrack needs.

3. Adobe Audition

Overview: Adobe Audition is a professional-grade audio editing software with a robust set of tools designed for high-quality sound production. It's part of Adobe's Creative Cloud suite, which means it comes with a subscription fee.

- **Pros**:
  - Advanced editing tools for precise control over every aspect of audio.
  - Supports multitrack editing and mixing, making it suitable for complex podcast productions.
  - Comprehensive noise reduction, restoration tools, and effects for professional-quality sound.
- **Cons**:
  - Subscription-based, with a monthly fee that can add up over time.
  - Requires a steeper learning curve, especially for beginners.
  - May be more powerful than necessary for simple podcast editing.
- **Special Features**: Adobe Audition offers industry-standard tools like spectral editing (which visually represents sound frequencies) and batch processing (editing multiple files at once). It also has excellent noise reduction capabilities and customizable effects.

Best for: Podcasters with experience or those aiming for professional, high-quality production. Ideal for more complex editing, detailed sound design, or multitrack projects.

Each of these software options has its strengths, so the right choice depends on your experience level, budget, and editing needs. For beginners, Audacity and GarageBand are excellent, user-friendly options, while Adobe Audition offers advanced features for those seeking professional-quality audio control. Whatever you choose, these tools provide a solid foundation for creating polished, engaging podcast episodes.

Budget-Friendly Options

Starting a podcast doesn't have to mean spending a lot on equipment and software. With the right budget-friendly tools, you can create high-quality audio without breaking the bank. Here are some affordable options for microphones, headphones, pop filters, and software that can help you achieve professional sound without a big investment.

1. Microphone

A good microphone is essential for clear audio, and there are several affordable options that deliver quality sound.

- **Audio-Technica ATR2100x-USB** ($99): This versatile microphone offers both USB and XLR connections, so you can use it as a beginner with USB and upgrade to XLR later if you decide to expand your setup. It provides crisp sound quality and is well-suited for voice recording.

- **Fifine K669B USB Microphone** ($30): A great budget option, the Fifine K669B is a USB microphone with decent sound quality for its price. It's easy to set up and works well for solo podcasting or casual interviews.

- **Samsung Q2U USB/XLR** ($70): Similar to the ATR2100x, the Samsung Q2U is a USB/XLR hybrid, providing great flexibility and solid audio quality for beginners.

Why it works: These microphones are cost-effective but offer sound quality that's good enough for podcasting, ensuring your voice sounds clear and professional.

2. Headphones

Good headphones help you monitor your audio and catch any issues during recording. Closed-back headphones are ideal for podcasting, as they minimize sound bleed.

- **OneOdio Studio Pro-10** ($35): These closed-back headphones offer good sound quality and comfort without the high price tag. They're popular among budget-conscious podcasters for their decent audio fidelity and sturdy build.

- **Audio-Technica ATH-M20x** ($50): A more affordable version of Audio-Technica's popular line, the ATH-M20x headphones provide clear sound and a comfortable fit, perfect for monitoring recordings on a budget.

Why it works: These budget headphones allow you to hear your recordings accurately, helping you catch issues like background noise or mic pops before they end up in your final audio.

3. Pop Filter

A pop filter is a simple but effective tool that reduces plosive sounds—those harsh "p" and "b" sounds that can distort your audio.

- **Aokeo Professional Pop Filter** ($10): A highly affordable and popular choice, this pop filter clips easily onto most microphone stands and does a great job of softening plosive sounds.

- **InnoGear Pop Filter** ($8): Another budget option, the InnoGear filter is double-layered to further reduce popping sounds, and it's highly adjustable for easy placement.

Why it works: Even a low-cost pop filter makes a noticeable difference in audio quality, softening harsh sounds and improving the clarity of your voice.

4. Boom Arm or Mic Stand

A boom arm or mic stand is helpful for positioning your microphone at the right height and angle, which can improve comfort and consistency in sound.

- **Neewer Adjustable Boom Arm** ($15): This affordable boom arm offers good flexibility for positioning your mic, and it clamps easily to most desks.

- **InnoGear Mic Stand** ($20): A reliable option with adjustable height, the InnoGear stand is perfect for podcasters who want a stable base for their microphone.

Why it works: Positioning your mic correctly helps maintain a consistent sound and prevents audio issues due to movement. These budget-friendly stands make it easy to set up a comfortable, reliable recording position.

5. Recording Software

There are several free or low-cost software options that provide solid recording and editing tools, perfect for podcasters starting out.

- **Audacity** (Free): Audacity is a free, open-source recording and editing software available for Windows, macOS, and Linux. It has all the basic tools you need to edit your podcast, including noise reduction and equalization.

- **GarageBand** (Free for Mac users): GarageBand is a user-friendly, multitrack audio editor pre-installed on most Apple devices. It's perfect for beginners who want to experiment with editing without a high learning curve.

- **Ocenaudio** (Free): A straightforward audio editor, Ocenaudio is compatible with Windows, macOS, and Linux. It's less feature-heavy than Audacity but easy to use, making it ideal for quick edits and simple adjustments.

Why it works: These free software options give beginners access to essential editing tools, enabling you to produce high-quality audio without investing in expensive software.

With this budget-friendly equipment and software, you can achieve high-quality audio that sounds professional. By investing in a solid USB microphone, affordable headphones, a pop filter, and free or low-cost recording software, you'll have everything you need to start your podcast without a big upfront cost. This setup ensures you're ready to record clear, polished episodes, allowing you to focus on creating great content without worrying about complex or costly gear.

Alex Reid

Chapter 5

Recording Your First Episode

Setting Up Your Recording Space

Creating a quiet, acoustically-friendly recording space at home doesn't require a professional studio, but a few simple adjustments can make a big difference in audio quality. The goal is to minimize background noise and reduce echo, both of which can be distracting to listeners.

First, choose a room that's naturally quiet and has minimal outside noise. Rooms with thick carpets, rugs, or plenty of soft furnishings are ideal because they absorb sound, reducing echo and reverb. Smaller rooms also tend to have less echo than large, open spaces. Avoid areas with hard surfaces like kitchens or bathrooms, as these can cause sound to bounce around.

To further improve your recording space, consider placing blankets or pillows around the room, especially on walls or windows that might reflect sound. If you're on a budget, you can even hang a thick blanket or comforter behind you or around your recording area to dampen any echo. Adding bookshelves, curtains, or even foam panels can also absorb sound effectively.

Finally, it's helpful to turn off any appliances or electronics that generate noise—this includes fans, air conditioners, and even fluorescent lights if they produce a hum. Consider recording at a time when your environment is naturally quieter, such as early in the morning or late at night. And, of course, make sure any pets or potential interruptions are kept at bay while you record.

By following these steps, you'll create a comfortable, quiet recording space that enhances the quality of your audio and provides a professional feel for your podcast, no studio required.

Tips for Clear Speaking

Clear, engaging speech is key to keeping listeners hooked on your podcast. Even if you have great content, how you deliver it makes all the difference. Here are some techniques to help you speak clearly, sound natural, and keep your audience engaged.

Start with vocal warm-ups to prepare your voice and prevent strain. Simple exercises like humming or deep breathing can help relax your vocal cords and improve clarity. Try saying tongue twisters to loosen up your mouth and improve pronunciation. For example, phrases like "red leather, yellow leather" or "unique New York" can get your mouth muscles ready for precise speech.

Reducing filler words like "uh," "um," "like," and "you know" helps you sound more confident and professional. A good trick is to pause instead of filling silence with these words. If you feel a filler word coming on, take a brief pause instead—this gives your mind a moment to catch up and allows you to refocus on your message. Practice this consciously, and over time, it'll become a habit.

Maintaining a conversational tone makes your podcast feel natural and approachable. Imagine you're speaking to a friend rather than an audience—this helps keep your tone warm and engaging. Avoid sounding overly scripted or formal; instead, let your personality come through. A helpful trick is to smile while you talk—it subtly changes your tone, making you sound friendlier and more relaxed.

By warming up, minimizing fillers, and keeping a conversational tone, you'll be well on your way to delivering clear and compelling podcast episodes that keep listeners coming back.

Recording Techniques

Getting your recording techniques right is essential for producing high-quality audio that keeps listeners engaged. Good techniques don't just improve sound quality—they also make the editing process smoother and save time in post-production. Here are some effective techniques for capturing clear, professional audio, including mic positioning, volume control, and handling interruptions.

Mic Positioning

Positioning your microphone correctly is one of the easiest ways to improve audio quality. Ideally, keep the microphone about 4–6 inches from your mouth and slightly off-center, which helps reduce plosive sounds (the hard "p" and "b" sounds that can cause audio spikes). You can also use a pop filter or foam cover to soften these sounds. The exact distance will depend on your microphone type, so test a few distances to find what works best. Positioning your mic this way creates a clear, warm sound and reduces the need for heavy editing.

Volume Control

Speaking at a consistent volume throughout your recording is key for a smooth listening experience. Adjust your microphone gain so that your voice is loud enough to capture detail without causing distortion. A general rule is to keep audio levels around -12 dB to -6 dB. This level gives you enough headroom, preventing clipping (distortion from loud peaks) and allowing you to adjust volume in post-production without losing quality. When speaking, maintain a steady distance from the mic to avoid sudden volume changes, especially if you tend to move or gesture while recording.

Minimizing Background Noise

Reducing background noise can make a huge difference in audio quality. Record in a quiet, controlled environment, preferably a room with carpeting or soft furnishings to absorb sound. Close doors and windows, turn off any fans or electronics that may hum, and ask household members to minimize noise. If you're in a space with unavoidable noise, consider using noise reduction tools in your editing software, but use them sparingly to avoid making your voice sound unnatural. The goal is to capture as clean a recording as possible so that you don't need to rely heavily on post-production fixes.

Handling Interruptions Smoothly

Even in a controlled setting, interruptions happen. If you make a mistake or experience an interruption, pause and restart the sentence or thought from a natural point. This will make editing much easier, as you'll have clean segments to work with and won't need to reconstruct sentences in post-production. Leave a few seconds of silence when restarting so that it's easier to spot in the editing timeline. This technique not only saves editing time but also helps maintain a natural flow in your speech.

Breath Control and Pace

Controlling your breathing and pace is essential for a smooth recording. Take measured breaths, especially before longer sentences, and try to speak at a relaxed pace to avoid sounding rushed. If you find yourself running out of breath mid-sentence, take a quick pause and restart the sentence. Breathing control not only improves audio quality but also makes your voice sound more confident and engaging.

Final Touch: Headphone Monitoring

Listening through headphones while recording allows you to hear exactly what your mic is capturing, helping you catch issues in real-time. Use closed-back headphones, which prevent sound from leaking into the microphone, and monitor your audio to make sure everything sounds clean and balanced. Monitoring helps you catch small issues like background noise, uneven volume, or mouth sounds before they become bigger problems in editing.

By mastering these recording techniques, you'll produce clearer, more professional audio with less post-production work. Each of these practices makes a noticeable impact on sound quality, giving your podcast that polished, engaging feel listeners enjoy.

Alex Reid

Chapter 6

Editing Like a Pro

Essential Editing Techniques

Editing is where your raw audio transforms into a polished, listener-ready episode. With just a few essential techniques, you can make your podcast sound seamless and professional. Here's a guide to some of the most effective editing techniques, including tips for making your edits sound natural.

1. Cutting and Trimming

Cutting and trimming help you remove any unnecessary parts of your recording, such as long pauses, stumbles, or repeated phrases. Start by listening through your recording and identifying sections that can be removed to improve flow. For instance, if there's a long pause while you gather your thoughts, cut it to keep the pace lively. Similarly, if you repeated a point or got off track, trim it out so that your episode stays focused.

When making cuts, aim to edit in places where natural pauses occur, like at the end of a sentence or paragraph. This makes the transition smoother and less noticeable to the listener. A useful tip is to use crossfade features (available in many editing programs) at the beginning and end of each cut, which helps to smooth any abrupt changes in background noise or tone.

2. Balancing Audio Levels

Balancing audio levels ensures that each speaker is equally audible and that the overall volume of the episode is consistent. Begin by adjusting the volume of each track so that everyone's voice is at a similar level. Pay attention to volume spikes, where someone might have spoken louder, and lower these areas to match the rest of the audio.

Many editors use "normalization" to bring the audio to a standard level, making it easier for listeners to hear without adjusting their volume. Another tool, "compression," can be helpful here as well; it reduces the volume of loud parts and raises quieter parts, creating a more balanced and consistent sound across the episode.

3. Reducing Background Noise

If you have any background noise in your recording, such as hums or faint sounds, noise reduction tools can help clean it up. Most audio software, like Audacity or Adobe Audition, has a "noise reduction" feature where you can capture a sample of the background noise and reduce it throughout the recording. Be cautious with this tool—overusing it can make your voice sound unnatural or "robotic."

4. Making Edits Sound Seamless and Natural

The key to great editing is making cuts sound as natural as possible. Pay attention to the flow of your speech, and avoid abrupt changes that can disrupt the listener's experience. One way to achieve seamless edits is by adding subtle fades between cuts, which softens the transition and keeps the audio smooth.

If you're working with multiple tracks (for example, in interviews), you can create a natural rhythm by slightly overlapping tracks where one person's response starts just as the other finishes speaking. This technique mimics a real-life conversation, helping it sound organic.

Using these essential editing techniques—cutting and trimming, balancing audio levels, reducing background noise, and blending edits naturally—will give your podcast a professional edge. With practice, you'll develop a feel for what sounds best and how to enhance your audio without over-editing, creating a podcast that's smooth, engaging, and enjoyable for listeners.

Adding Music and Effects

Incorporating background music and sound effects can add depth, energy, and emotion to your podcast. Music sets the tone for your show and creates a memorable atmosphere, while sound effects can enhance storytelling and engagement. Here's how to use them effectively and keep your audio professional and engaging.

1. Choosing the Right Background Music

When selecting music, think about the mood you want to set. Do you want an upbeat, energetic vibe? Or perhaps a calming, thoughtful atmosphere? The right background music can enhance your podcast's theme and keep listeners engaged. For example, upbeat music can bring energy to intros and outros, while softer tracks work well in storytelling or reflective segments.

Make sure to use royalty-free or licensed music to avoid copyright issues. There are many platforms that offer affordable or free options, like **Epidemic Sound**, **Artlist**,

Free Music Archive, and **YouTube Audio Library**. Some sites require a subscription, while others let you purchase individual tracks or offer free downloads with proper attribution.

2. Using Sound Effects to Enhance Storytelling

Sound effects are especially useful in narrative or interview-based podcasts. They can bring scenes to life and make stories feel more immersive. For instance, adding subtle background sounds like birds chirping or a coffee shop's ambiance can transport listeners to a specific setting. If you're explaining a process or guiding listeners through steps, simple cues like a "ding" to indicate completion can keep the episode engaging and help listeners follow along.

Just as with music, ensure you use royalty-free sound effects. Websites like **Freesound**, **SoundBible**, and **ZapSplat** offer a range of free effects that you can download and use with attribution or license, depending on the site's terms.

3. Mixing Music and Effects Smoothly

Effective mixing makes sure your music and sound effects complement, rather than overpower, your main audio. Here are some tips for blending them seamlessly:

- **Keep Volume Balanced**: Background music should enhance, not compete with, your voice. Lower the volume of music tracks during narration so that your voice remains clear. A good rule of thumb is to keep music around 15-25% volume relative to your voice.

- **Use Fades for Smooth Transitions**: Start and end background music with gradual fades, rather than abrupt starts and stops. This creates a smoother experience for listeners and signals transitions in the episode.

- **Place Effects Strategically**: Sound effects are most effective when used sparingly. Use them to punctuate important moments or enhance specific scenes, rather than overloading each segment. This keeps effects impactful without overwhelming your listeners.

- **Layer Thoughtfully**: If you're using both music and effects, be mindful of how they interact. For example, avoid placing busy sound effects over music that already has a lot of movement or beats. Instead, use simpler music with minimal instruments when layering multiple audio elements.

4. Final Check: Listening with Fresh Ears

After mixing, take a break and then listen back with fresh ears, ideally using headphones. This will help you catch any imbalances in volume or moments where effects might distract from your main audio. Adjust as needed, ensuring that your music and effects support the episode rather than taking over.

By choosing the right music, incorporating effects purposefully, and mixing with care, you'll create a podcast that's immersive and polished, enhancing the listener experience without distracting from your message. With practice, adding music and effects will become an easy and effective way to bring your episodes to life.

Final Touches

The final steps in editing your podcast are all about refining your audio to ensure it sounds as polished and professional as possible. These last touches—like audio polishing, equalization, and volume leveling—can make a noticeable difference in the overall quality of your episode. Here's a step-by-step guide to give your podcast that finishing touch, along with essential quality checks before publishing.

1. Audio Polishing

Audio polishing involves making small adjustments that enhance the clarity and smoothness of your recording. Start by removing any last bits of background noise that may still be present. Use your software's noise reduction tool to do this carefully—just enough to reduce unwanted sounds without making the audio sound unnatural or "processed."

Next, consider adding subtle effects like reverb or echo to make the audio feel richer, but use these sparingly. For spoken-word podcasts, too much reverb can make the voice sound distant or hollow, so it's best to keep these effects minimal.

---

2. Equalization (EQ)

Equalization, or EQ, is the process of adjusting different frequency ranges in your audio. For podcasting, EQ can help make your voice sound clearer, warmer, or more balanced. Most podcasts benefit from the following basic adjustments:

- **Low-End Roll-Off**: Cut the very low frequencies (below 80-100 Hz) to remove any rumble or background noise.

- **Boost Mid-Range**: Gently boost the mid-range frequencies (around 300-500 Hz) to make your voice sound fuller and more present.

- **Add Brightness**: A slight boost in the high frequencies (around 3-5 kHz) can add clarity and crispness to your voice, making it easier to understand.

Adjust these settings carefully, listening as you go, to achieve a natural, balanced sound. Many editing programs have presets for spoken voice that can help you start, and you can fine-tune from there.

3. Volume Leveling

Consistent volume levels are crucial for a smooth listening experience. Leveling ensures that your voice, music, and any other audio elements have balanced volumes, so listeners don't need to constantly adjust their volume. Use the following techniques:

- **Normalization**: Most software has a "normalize" feature that can automatically bring your audio to a standard level (often around -3 dB), which is ideal for podcasting. This will make your audio loud enough without causing distortion.

- **Compression**: Compression smooths out volume fluctuations by reducing the loudest parts and raising the quieter parts. Apply a gentle compression setting, which will help your audio sound consistent without making it sound overly processed. Many programs have presets, like "light compression" or "speech," that work well for podcast voices.

4. Quality Checks Before Publishing

Once you've made these final adjustments, it's time to do a last check to make sure everything sounds professional. Here are some key quality checks:

- **Listen on Different Devices**: Play your episode through headphones, computer speakers, and a smartphone to ensure it sounds good across different devices. This helps you catch any imbalances that might be noticeable on certain speakers.

- **Check for Consistency**: Make sure all sections have a similar volume level and that any music or sound effects are balanced with the voice. Listen carefully for any abrupt cuts, transitions, or unexpected noises.

- **Confirm File Format**: For most podcast platforms, exporting your file as an MP3 (at 128-192 kbps) is standard. This format provides good audio quality at a manageable file size.

By taking these final steps, you're ensuring your episode has a clean, polished sound that's enjoyable for listeners. With practice, these final touches will become a quick and routine part of your editing process, giving each episode a professional edge and making your podcast stand out.

Chapter 7

Publishing Your Podcast

Hosting Platforms

Choosing the right hosting platform is a crucial step in getting your podcast out to the world. A podcast host stores your audio files and generates an RSS feed, which allows podcast directories like Apple Podcasts, Spotify, and Google Podcasts to access and display your episodes. Here's an overview of popular podcast hosting platforms, including their pricing, storage limits, and unique features.

---

1. Anchor

Overview: Anchor is a free, user-friendly podcast hosting platform owned by Spotify. It's popular among beginners for its simplicity and integration with Spotify.

- **Pricing**: Free.

- **Storage Limits**: Unlimited storage and episodes.

- **Unique Features**:

- o **Easy-to-Use Interface**: Anchor's simple dashboard allows you to record, edit, and publish episodes directly within the platform.

- o **Monetization Options**: Anchor provides built-in monetization tools like listener support and sponsorships.

- o **Analytics**: Basic analytics are available, including episode plays, listener demographics, and platform distribution.

- o **Automatic Distribution**: Anchor automatically distributes your podcast to major platforms like Apple Podcasts and Spotify.

Best For: Beginners and those looking for a free, easy-to-use platform with basic tools and direct access to Spotify's audience.

2. Podbean

Overview: Podbean is a versatile hosting platform with a range of pricing tiers, making it suitable for both beginners and more advanced podcasters. It includes monetization tools, detailed analytics, and a customizable podcast website.

- **Pricing**:
  - o **Basic**: Free (with limited storage and bandwidth).
  - o **Unlimited Audio**: $9/month (includes unlimited storage and bandwidth).
  - o **Unlimited Plus**: $29/month (includes advanced monetization features).
- **Storage Limits**: Unlimited storage on paid plans.
- **Unique Features**:

o **Customizable Website**: Podbean provides a free website with customizable themes to help you promote your show.

o **Live Streaming**: Podbean allows live-streaming podcasts, where listeners can tune in live and interact in real-time.

o **Monetization Options**: Includes tools for ad insertion, premium content, and crowdfunding options.

o **Detailed Analytics**: Offers in-depth analytics on downloads, listener behavior, and geographical data.

Best For: Podcasters looking for a customizable hosting solution with a range of monetization options and advanced analytics.

---

3. Libsyn

Overview: Libsyn (short for Liberated Syndication) is one of the oldest and most trusted podcast hosting platforms. Known for its reliability, it's widely used by seasoned podcasters and offers detailed analytics and custom distribution options.

- **Pricing**:

  o Starts at $5/month for 50 MB of storage.

  o Plans with more storage range from $15/month to $75/month.

- **Storage Limits**: Storage is monthly, so you have a set amount each month rather than an overall limit. Higher plans offer more monthly storage.

- **Unique Features**:

- o **Customizable RSS Feed**: Provides more control over your RSS feed, which is useful for advanced users.

- o **Libsyn Publisher Hub**: A WordPress plugin that integrates with Libsyn, allowing you to manage episodes directly from your WordPress site.

- o **Analytics**: Offers comprehensive analytics, including detailed download stats, audience demographics, and device breakdowns.

- o **Distribution Network**: Provides distribution to major podcast platforms and social media integration to help broaden your reach.

Best For: Experienced podcasters or those seeking control over their podcast feed, advanced distribution options, and comprehensive analytics.

Each of these platforms has its strengths, so the best one for you depends on your needs, budget, and podcasting goals. Anchor is ideal for beginners who want a straightforward, free option with basic features and easy integration with Spotify. Podbean offers a balance of affordability, customization, and monetization, making it suitable for podcasters seeking a scalable solution. Libsyn, with its robust features and control, is perfect for advanced users who want a reliable host with detailed analytics and advanced options.

No matter which host you choose, these platforms make it easy to publish and share your podcast, giving you the tools and support to grow your audience.

Submitting to Platforms

Once your podcast is ready, submitting it to major directories like Apple Podcasts, Spotify, and Google Podcasts will make it accessible to a wide audience. Each platform has slightly different requirements, so here's a streamlined guide on how to submit to each one.

To submit your podcast to **Apple Podcasts**, first ensure you have an Apple ID. Apple Podcasts requires an RSS feed that includes essential metadata: title, description, cover art (minimum 1400 x 1400 pixels in JPG or PNG format), and at least one published episode. Once your RSS feed is ready, log into Apple Podcasts Connect with your Apple ID. From there, paste your RSS feed link, and Apple will validate it to confirm all metadata requirements are met. If everything is in order, click "Submit." Approval usually takes a few days, but Apple will notify you via email once your podcast is live.

For **Spotify**, the submission process is straightforward. Visit Spotify for Podcasters and log in or create a Spotify account. Once logged in, click on "Get Started" and paste your RSS feed URL. Spotify will request some basic information, such as podcast category and language. Like Apple, Spotify will validate your feed to ensure it includes all required information. Once submitted, podcasts often go live on Spotify within a few hours, though it can sometimes take up to a day.

Submitting to **Google Podcasts** involves using Google Podcasts Manager. Log in with a Google account and paste your RSS feed URL. Google will send a verification email to the email address associated with your feed, so ensure that your contact email in the feed is accurate. After verification, Google will add your podcast to its directory, though it may take a few days for your podcast to appear in search results. Google Podcasts doesn't have as many specific requirements for artwork or metadata, as it primarily relies on your RSS feed's existing information.

Each platform has its own timeline for approval, so be prepared for slight variations. Once your podcast is submitted to these directories, it will be accessible to listeners across devices, making it easy for them to subscribe and enjoy your content.

Writing Engaging Descriptions

Crafting a compelling podcast description is essential for attracting listeners and making your show easy to find on platforms and search engines. Your description should be concise yet engaging, giving potential listeners a clear sense of what your podcast offers and why it's worth their time. Here's how to write descriptions that draw people in and improve discoverability.

Start by summarizing the core theme of your podcast in a single, clear sentence. Think of this as your "elevator pitch"— what makes your show unique? For example, instead of saying, "A podcast about personal finance," try something more specific like, "A no-nonsense guide to mastering your money, packed with practical tips and inspiring interviews." This approach instantly tells listeners what to expect and emphasizes the unique angle of your podcast.

Use keywords naturally throughout your description to help improve search engine optimization (SEO). Think about terms your ideal listener might search for and incorporate them in a natural, engaging way. If your podcast is about fitness for beginners, phrases like "beginner fitness tips," "home workouts," and "easy fitness routines" could be helpful. Remember, many podcast platforms, as well as Google, index these keywords, so well-chosen terms can make your show more discoverable.

Don't forget to highlight the value listeners will get from each episode. Instead of only listing topics, emphasize what people will gain, such as actionable advice, expert insights, or entertaining stories. For example, "Join us every week for expert advice on fitness, personal stories of transformation, and easy-to-follow workouts to help you stay motivated." This approach connects with readers by focusing on the benefits and keeps your tone inviting.

Finally, end with a call to action (CTA) that encourages listeners to subscribe, follow, or tune in to the latest episode. You could say something like, "Subscribe now to start your fitness journey with us, and get inspired every week!" A friendly CTA gives potential listeners that extra nudge to click "subscribe" or "follow."

With a clear summary, relevant keywords, and an engaging tone, your podcast description will not only inform but also attract your ideal listeners, making it easier for them to discover and connect with your show.

Alex Reid

Chapter 8

Building Your Audience

Marketing Strategies

Growing your podcast audience requires strategic promotion across multiple channels. A strong marketing approach combines social media, email marketing, and collaborations with others in the podcasting world. Here's how to leverage each of these methods effectively to reach and engage listeners.

Social media is one of the most powerful tools for promoting your podcast. Start by choosing platforms where your target audience is most active. For instance, Instagram and Twitter are ideal for building a general following, while LinkedIn may be more appropriate for business-focused podcasts. Regularly post about upcoming episodes, behind-the-scenes content, or highlights from recent shows. Use relevant hashtags to increase your visibility and join conversations in your niche. Short video or audio clips from episodes work well as teasers, giving followers a taste of what to expect. Don't forget to engage directly with your followers—reply to comments, ask questions, and encourage listeners to share their thoughts.

This interaction helps foster a sense of community around your podcast.

Email Marketing is another effective strategy for audience building. Start a mailing list and invite listeners to subscribe through your website or social media. Send regular updates with episode announcements, bonus content, and exclusive previews to keep your audience engaged. Email newsletters allow you to share more detailed content, such as show notes or summaries of past episodes, which can be particularly useful for loyal listeners who want to dive deeper. Segmenting your audience based on their interests can also help you deliver targeted content, improving engagement rates. Consistency is key—sending updates regularly, like weekly or bi-weekly, keeps your podcast top of mind for subscribers.

Collaborating with Other Podcasters can introduce your show to a new audience. Reach out to podcasters in similar or complementary niches and propose a guest swap or a joint episode. For instance, if your podcast is about wellness, collaborating with a mental health podcaster could bring fresh insights and attract new listeners interested in both topics. Guest appearances on other podcasts are also a great way to showcase your expertise to an audience that's already interested in the type of content you create. When collaborating, be sure to cross-promote on social media and provide links so that listeners can easily find and subscribe to your show.

Combining these marketing strategies—social media engagement, email marketing, and collaborations—helps you reach new listeners, engage with your existing audience, and build a loyal community around your podcast. By consistently promoting your show and connecting with your audience, you'll see steady growth and greater listener engagement over time.

Social Media Promotion

Social media is a powerful tool for growing your podcast audience, helping you reach new listeners and build a community around your show. To get the most out of social media, focus on choosing the right platforms, developing an effective posting strategy, and actively engaging with your followers. Here's how to leverage social media for maximum podcast growth.

Choosing the Right Platforms is the first step. Think about where your target audience spends the most time. If your podcast focuses on visual topics, like travel or cooking, Instagram or TikTok can be effective for sharing photo and video content. For more conversational or discussion-driven topics, Twitter is ideal for joining ongoing conversations and building a network through retweets and replies. LinkedIn works well for business or career-oriented podcasts, where professionals are likely to engage with industry content. Don't feel like you need to be on every platform; focus on 1-2 where your audience is most active.

Developing a Posting Strategy is essential to keep your content fresh and engaging. A good mix of content types can help you capture attention and encourage engagement. Share episode highlights, short video or audio clips, quotes from guests, and behind-the-scenes content to give followers a taste of what to expect from your podcast. Posting regularly is key to staying visible, so aim to post 3-4 times a week on your primary platform. Use platform-specific features, such as Instagram Stories or Twitter Threads, to keep your content interactive. For instance, using Instagram Stories for polls or question stickers allows you to engage followers directly and get feedback on what they'd like to hear next.

Engaging with Followers is crucial for building a loyal audience. Social media isn't just about broadcasting; it's a conversation. Respond to comments, like and share posts that mention your podcast, and ask questions to encourage discussion. This interaction shows your followers that you value their feedback and are interested in what they have to say. Engage with similar accounts or communities in your niche as well; commenting on and sharing their content builds connections that can lead to future collaborations or shared audiences. User-generated content, such as listener reviews or episode feedback, is a great way to showcase your community. Encourage followers to tag you in posts about the podcast, and feature their comments or stories on your page as a way to recognize and celebrate your listeners.

By focusing on the right platforms, posting valuable and varied content, and actively engaging with your audience, you'll build a vibrant online community that's invested in your podcast. Social media can be a powerful engine for growth when you use it to connect with listeners and make them feel like part of your journey.

Engaging Your Listeners

Building a loyal listener base requires more than just creating good content—it's about fostering a sense of community and making listeners feel involved in the podcast. Engaging your audience encourages them to keep coming back, spread the word, and feel personally connected to your show. Here are some effective ways to deepen listener engagement, encourage feedback, and create a strong, interactive community around your podcast.

1. Invite Feedback and Encourage Interaction

Encourage listeners to share their thoughts on episodes by inviting them to leave comments on social media, send messages, or email feedback. Prompt listeners with questions or specific calls for input at the end of each episode, like, "Let us know your thoughts on today's topic! Reach out on Twitter or Instagram, or send us a voice message!" You can also use polls and question boxes on platforms like Instagram Stories to gather quick feedback. By making this a routine, listeners know their input is valued and are more likely to contribute.

2. Encourage Reviews and Ratings

Positive reviews and ratings not only help improve your podcast's visibility but also serve as endorsements that can attract new listeners. At the end of an episode, ask listeners to leave a review if they enjoyed the content. You can add a personal touch by explaining how their support helps the show grow. As an incentive, consider doing a monthly shout-out where you read a few listener reviews on the show or feature them on your social media pages. This recognition shows that you appreciate their support, which can encourage more listeners to leave reviews.

3. Create a Space for Ongoing Interaction

Having a dedicated space where listeners can interact with each other, as well as with you, builds community and keeps people engaged between episodes. Consider starting a private Facebook group, Discord server, or even a subreddit where listeners can discuss episodes, share ideas, and connect with others who enjoy the show. These groups offer a space for deeper interaction, allow listeners to build relationships, and give you valuable insights into what resonates with your audience.

4. Host Q&A or Listener-Centric Episodes

Devote occasional episodes to listener questions or topics they've requested. Collect questions through email, social media, or your community groups, and feature them in a Q&A episode. By addressing listener-submitted questions or topics, you're showing that their voices matter and that you're responsive to their interests. These listener-focused episodes can also add variety to your show and help you explore topics that are directly relevant to your audience.

5. Use Giveaways and Contests

Giveaways and contests are fun ways to boost engagement and give back to your listeners. Offer something relevant, like podcast merchandise, a free resource, or even a guest appearance on the show. You could, for example, run a contest where listeners are entered by sharing their favorite episode on social media, tagging your podcast, and leaving a review. This approach encourages them to promote your show while feeling appreciated and excited to participate.

6. Recognize and Appreciate Your Listeners

Shout-outs or mentions are simple but effective ways to acknowledge your listeners. You might share a listener's story, read a thoughtful review, or thank followers by name on an episode. This personal touch shows your appreciation and strengthens the bond between you and your audience. Even something as simple as responding to listener messages on social media with a personalized thank-you can make listeners feel seen and valued.

By encouraging interaction, building a community space, and showing appreciation, you can create an environment where listeners feel like part of your podcast journey. This approach not only helps build loyalty but also fosters a community that supports and promotes your show, leading to sustainable growth and a more engaged audience.

Chapter 9

Monetizing Your Podcast

Sponsorships and Ads

Monetizing your podcast through sponsorships and ads can be a rewarding way to generate income, but it's essential to balance revenue with maintaining your audience's trust. Here's how to attract sponsors, incorporate ads effectively, and keep listeners engaged without compromising your podcast's integrity.

1. Attracting Sponsorships

To attract sponsors, start by building a consistent listener base, as sponsors are interested in reaching audiences that are loyal and engaged. Even with a smaller but dedicated audience, you can attract sponsors in a specific niche who value quality over quantity. Reach out to brands aligned with your podcast's theme or audience interests. For instance, if your podcast covers fitness, approach companies that sell health products, workout gear, or supplements. Craft a professional pitch that includes your listener demographics, average download numbers, and examples of audience engagement, as well as what unique value you can offer to their brand.

You can also join podcast advertising networks like Podcorn, Midroll, or AdvertiseCast, which connect podcasters with potential sponsors. These networks help simplify the process of finding and negotiating with sponsors, often taking a small commission in exchange.

2. Choosing the Right Ad Formats

Podcast ads generally come in three main formats:

- **Pre-roll Ads** (15-30 seconds): Placed at the beginning of an episode, pre-roll ads capture listeners' attention early. They're usually brief, so they work well for concise, brand-focused messages.

- **Mid-roll Ads** (60 seconds): These ads run in the middle of an episode and typically generate the highest rates due to listener retention during this time. Mid-roll ads allow for more in-depth messaging, so they're ideal for longer product explanations or personal endorsements.

- **Post-roll Ads** (15-30 seconds): Placed at the end of an episode, post-roll ads work well for call-to-action messages, though they typically have lower rates as some listeners may tune out before the episode finishes.

Consider offering a mix of ad formats to give sponsors options and to balance ad load within your episodes. Ideally, aim to keep ad time to no more than 2-3 minutes total per episode to avoid overwhelming listeners.

3. Setting Rates

Podcast ad rates are typically calculated on a CPM (cost per thousand impressions) basis. Average rates vary depending on factors like audience size and engagement, but a general starting point for podcasts is around $18-$25 CPM for a 30-second ad and $25-$50 CPM for a 60-second ad. As your podcast grows and your engagement rates improve, you can increase these rates or negotiate more flexible terms.

For smaller or niche podcasts, you might consider charging a flat rate per episode rather than CPM, especially if your audience is highly targeted. It's also possible to offer package deals where sponsors commit to multiple episodes, giving them a discount while securing steady revenue.

4. Maintaining Audience Trust

Trust is critical when incorporating ads. Your listeners tune in for valuable content, and they'll appreciate transparent, authentic ad placements that feel aligned with your podcast. One effective approach is to focus on sponsors whose products or services you've personally used or genuinely recommend. This allows you to speak authentically and naturally in your ad reads, making them more like endorsements than generic ads.

Integrate ads smoothly into your episodes by reading them yourself in your regular tone, as this can help ads feel less intrusive. For example, if you're doing a mid-roll ad, transition with a natural segue that connects the ad to your content, like, "Speaking of productivity, I've been using [sponsor's product] to stay organized, and it's been a game-changer."

Be upfront with your audience about sponsorships by saying that ads help support the show. When listeners understand that ad revenue allows you to keep creating free content, they're more likely to be receptive to ads and continue tuning in.

By choosing sponsors carefully, structuring ads thoughtfully, and prioritizing authenticity, you'll be able to monetize your podcast effectively while keeping your audience's trust. This balance not only helps sustain your podcast financially but also ensures that listeners remain loyal and engaged.

Building a Podcast Brand

Developing a recognizable podcast brand is essential for standing out in a crowded field and creating a loyal audience. Your brand is more than just a logo or tagline—it's the personality, voice, and visual identity that your audience connects with. Here's how to build a strong podcast brand with key elements like a logo, tagline, and consistent visuals across platforms.

1. Crafting a Memorable Logo

Your logo is often the first visual element people notice about your podcast, so it should be memorable and reflective of your show's tone. When designing a logo, keep it simple, bold, and legible, even at small sizes (think of how it'll look on a mobile screen). Use colors and fonts that match your podcast's vibe— bright colors and modern fonts work well for upbeat, lighthearted shows, while a more muted color palette and classic fonts might suit a serious, investigative podcast.

If you're not a designer, there are plenty of resources to help. You can use design platforms like **Canva** or **Adobe Spark**, which offer templates and customization options, or hire a designer on a freelance platform like **Fiverr** or **99designs** to create a unique logo that captures your podcast's essence.

2. Creating a Compelling Tagline

A tagline is a brief, catchy phrase that sums up what listeners can expect from your podcast. A strong tagline communicates your podcast's value in just a few words, helping potential listeners instantly understand your show. For instance, a fitness podcast's tagline might be "Your Weekly Workout Companion," while a history podcast's could be "Exploring the Stories Behind the Facts."

To create a great tagline, think about what makes your podcast unique and what your audience is looking for. Keep it short—ideally under 10 words—and make it intriguing. A well-crafted tagline can grab attention and convey a sense of your podcast's content and tone in a flash.

3. Defining Your Podcast's Personality and Tone

Your podcast brand also includes the way you communicate with your audience. Think about the tone you want to convey—is it friendly and casual, educational and professional, or maybe humorous and irreverent? This tone should come through consistently in everything from your episode scripts to your social media posts. For example, if your podcast is about technology news, your tone might be informative and slightly formal, whereas a pop culture podcast could have a more casual, conversational vibe.

4. Using Consistent Visuals Across Platforms

Consistency is key to building a recognizable brand. Use the same colors, fonts, and logo across all platforms where your podcast is present, including your website, social media profiles, and podcast directories. This consistency helps reinforce your brand visually, so when people see your posts, they immediately associate them with your podcast.

For example, if your logo uses a dark blue and white color scheme, carry those colors into your social media graphics, website, and any marketing materials. Canva is an excellent tool for creating visually consistent templates, as it allows you to save custom colors and fonts.

5. Writing an Engaging Show Description

Your show description is an important branding element that communicates your podcast's value to potential listeners. Write a description that is true to your brand's voice and highlights what makes your show unique. Include a mix of keywords that represent your podcast's theme, as these will help improve discoverability on platforms and search engines.

6. Establishing a Social Media Presence

Social media is an extension of your podcast brand, and it's where you can interact with listeners in real-time. Make your profiles on platforms like Instagram, Twitter, and Facebook match your podcast brand visually and tonally. Create consistent, engaging posts that reflect your show's personality, whether that's humorous memes, behind-the-scenes photos, or educational content.

7. Branding Your Episodes

To reinforce your brand in every episode, consider using a short, recognizable intro and outro with background music that matches your podcast's tone. Your intro can include a brief tagline, the show name, and a quick preview of the episode, helping listeners instantly recognize your podcast.

8. Building Your Website as a Central Hub

If you create a website for your podcast, ensure it's an extension of your brand. Include your logo, tagline, and a matching color scheme. Your website can act as a central hub where listeners can access all episodes, learn more about the show, and find links to your social media and platforms. A cohesive website strengthens your brand and makes it easy for listeners to find and share your content.

By creating a consistent, memorable brand across all elements—logo, tagline, tone, visuals, and interactions—you'll make your podcast stand out, connect more easily with listeners, and leave a lasting impression. Your brand is what keeps listeners coming back, and with a thoughtful approach, it can turn casual listeners into dedicated fans.

Staying Consistent

Consistency is one of the most important factors in growing and sustaining a podcast audience. A predictable release schedule builds trust with listeners and keeps them coming back. Here's how to maintain a steady release schedule through smart planning, batching episodes, and prioritizing quality over quantity.

1. Plan Ahead with a Content Calendar

Creating a content calendar helps you stay organized and gives you a clear roadmap for upcoming episodes. Plan out your episodes at least a month in advance, considering any seasonal topics or special events you may want to align with. A content calendar allows you to visualize your release schedule, ensuring that you have topics and ideas lined up. When you know what's coming, it's easier to prepare content in advance and avoid last-minute scrambles. As part of your planning, decide on specific release days and times, so your audience knows exactly when to expect new episodes.

2. Batch Record and Edit Episodes

Batching is a game-changer when it comes to maintaining consistency. Set aside dedicated time to record multiple episodes in one session, especially if they're shorter episodes or if you're planning a series. After recording, you can also batch-edit the episodes, which saves time and keeps you ahead of schedule. Batching not only frees up time for other tasks but also provides a buffer in case unexpected events prevent you from recording or editing on short notice. This way, you always have content ready to go, helping you stick to your schedule even during busy periods.

3. Set Realistic Goals for Your Schedule

While it's tempting to aim for a high-frequency release schedule, choose a pace that's manageable long-term. For example, if producing an episode every week feels overwhelming, consider releasing biweekly instead. It's better to commit to a schedule you can maintain than to overextend and risk burnout. Many successful podcasts grow consistently with biweekly or even monthly releases, so pick a frequency that balances your availability with your content goals. Once you commit, stick to it, as listeners appreciate consistency.

4. Prioritize Content Quality

Staying consistent doesn't mean compromising quality. If you're ever faced with the choice of rushing an episode to meet a deadline or delaying it for a few days to improve quality, always choose quality. Your audience will forgive a delay, but they may lose interest if episodes feel rushed or poorly produced. Remember, every episode reflects your brand. Consistency builds trust, but so does quality content that keeps listeners engaged and excited for the next release.

5. Use Scheduling Tools and Reminders

Scheduling tools like Google Calendar or dedicated podcast project management apps, such as Trello or Notion, can keep you on track. Use reminders and deadlines to manage each phase of production—research, scripting, recording, editing, and promoting. Many podcast hosting platforms also allow you to schedule episodes to go live automatically, so you can upload and schedule episodes ahead of time without worrying about the release day.

6. Build a Content Buffer

Whenever possible, maintain a buffer of pre-recorded, edited episodes. Having 1-3 episodes ready to go allows you to manage your workload effectively and adds flexibility in case you need a break or face unexpected disruptions. A content buffer ensures that your release schedule won't be affected by temporary challenges and keeps your audience engaged without interruption.

By planning ahead, batching your work, setting realistic goals, and maintaining a focus on quality, you can build a consistent release schedule that enhances your podcast's reliability and keeps your audience engaged. Consistency shows listeners you're committed to the podcast, and over time, it will help grow a loyal listener base.

Alex Reid

Chapter 11

Legal Aspects of Podcasting

Copyright and Permissions

Understanding copyright is essential to producing a podcast that respects legal guidelines and avoids infringement. Copyright laws protect original works like music, literature, and art, ensuring that creators control how their work is used. Here's a straightforward guide to copyright basics and tips on avoiding infringement when using music, quotes, or other content.

1. Music and Sound Effects

Using music or sound effects in your podcast requires special attention, as most music is copyrighted. To use a song legally, you must have permission from the copyright holder, which typically involves paying for a license. Many podcasters opt for royalty-free music, which can be used without ongoing fees once a license is purchased. Sites like **Epidemic Sound**, **Artlist**, and **PremiumBeat** offer royalty-free music for a one-time fee or subscription, providing access to music you can legally use. Additionally, there are free music libraries, such as **YouTube Audio Library** and **Freesound**, where you can find public domain or Creative Commons-licensed music.

If you want to use music with a **Creative Commons license**, make sure to check the specific terms, as some licenses allow only non-commercial use or require you to credit the creator. Look for music licensed as **CC BY** (attribution required) or **CCo** (public domain, no attribution required) for the most freedom of use. Always credit the artist as specified in the license if required.

2. Using Quotes and Excerpts

In general, short quotes or excerpts may fall under **fair use**, especially if used for purposes like commentary, criticism, or education. However, fair use can be a gray area, as it depends on factors like the purpose and length of the quote, and whether it impacts the original work's value. To be safe, keep quotes brief, use only as much as is necessary to make your point, and provide context for the quote within your own content.

When quoting from books, articles, or speeches, always credit the source, even if it's in the public domain. This transparency not only respects the original creator but also adds credibility to your podcast. If you plan to use a significant portion of someone's work, it's best to reach out for permission to avoid any issues.

3. Images and Artwork

Any visuals used to promote your podcast, such as episode cover art, should also follow copyright guidelines. Avoid using images from Google or social media without permission, as these are often protected. Instead, use royalty-free images from sites like **Unsplash**, **Pexels**, or **Pixabay**, which offer high-quality images that can be used without copyright concerns. For a unique look, consider creating your own artwork or hiring a designer.

4. Understanding Public Domain and Creative Commons

Content in the **public domain** is free for anyone to use without restrictions, as it's not protected by copyright. Examples include works by long-deceased authors and creators, such as classic literature or historical speeches. Creative Commons is another useful resource, providing different levels of permissions for use. Content marked **CC0** or as public domain is free for any use, while other Creative Commons licenses (such as CC BY or CC BY-SA) may require attribution or limit usage to non-commercial projects.

5. Asking for Permission When in Doubt

If you're unsure about using a piece of content, the safest route is to ask for permission. Contact the creator or rights holder and explain how you intend to use their work. Many creators are open to allowing usage, especially when credit is given, but getting written permission protects you legally. Having permission is especially important if you're using content that will be central to your podcast's theme, such as a recurring song or significant quotes.

By understanding copyright basics, using royalty-free resources, and crediting creators, you can avoid infringement while creating a podcast that respects other people's work. Taking these steps not only keeps your podcast legally compliant but also shows respect for the creative community, fostering a positive environment for creators and listeners alike.

Music and Sound Effects Usage

Adding music and sound effects to your podcast can enhance the listener experience, but it's essential to use these elements legally to avoid copyright issues. Royalty-free music and sound effects are popular choices for podcasters, as they're accessible, legal, and affordable. Here's a guide on finding and using royalty-free audio, including the licenses and permissions you need.

Understanding Royalty-Free vs. Copyright-Free

Royalty-free music means that, once you pay a one-time fee or subscription, you can use the music without paying ongoing royalties or fees. However, the copyright is still held by the creator or distributor, so you must follow the licensing terms they provide. This differs from "copyright-free" or "public domain" music, which has no copyright restrictions and can be used freely. When using royalty-free music, always read the licensing terms carefully to understand how and where you can use the music.

Finding Royalty-Free Music and Sound Effects

There are several reliable sites where you can find quality royalty-free music and sound effects:

- **Epidemic Sound**: Offers a vast library of music and sound effects for a subscription fee. The license covers both personal and commercial use, allowing you to use tracks on your podcast without additional royalties.

- **Artlist**: Provides high-quality music with an unlimited license for a flat fee. Artlist's license allows use across multiple platforms, including podcasts, social media, and YouTube.

- **PremiumBeat**: Charges a one-time fee per track and offers a broad selection of professional music.

PremiumBeat's license allows for both personal and commercial use, ideal for podcasts.

- **YouTube Audio Library**: Free for YouTube content and other projects, including podcasts. Be sure to check each track's attribution requirements, as some may need you to credit the artist.

- **Freesound**: Offers a variety of sound effects with different licenses. Some tracks require attribution (CC BY), while others are public domain (CCo). Always check the license associated with each sound effect to confirm permissions.

These platforms provide a range of options at different price points, and each license may have specific terms, so it's essential to review them carefully.

Types of Licenses and Permissions

When using royalty-free audio, the license type determines how and where you can use it. Here's a quick overview of common license types you may encounter:

- **Personal License**: Limits usage to personal projects. This is usually not suitable for podcasts intended for public or commercial distribution.

- **Commercial License**: Allows use in publicly available or revenue-generating content, including podcasts. Most royalty-free sites provide commercial licenses, which are ideal for podcast use.

- **Creative Commons Licenses**: Tracks on sites like Freesound often use Creative Commons (CC) licenses, which may require attribution. Common types include:

  - **CC BY**: Allows free use with attribution to the creator.

- ○ **CC BY-NC**: Allows free use for non-commercial projects only, with attribution required.

- ○ **CCo**: Public domain; no attribution required, free for all uses.

Always check if a track requires attribution and, if so, include the artist's name and source in your podcast credits or episode description. When using Creative Commons tracks, make sure the license type aligns with your podcast's purpose, particularly if it's monetized.

Best Practices for Legal and Proper Usage

To ensure you're using music and sound effects legally:

- **Read License Agreements Carefully**: Each platform has unique terms for using their music. Ensure the license allows for podcast use and whether attribution is needed.

- **Document Your Licenses**: Keep records of any licenses or permissions for the music and sound effects you use. This documentation can protect you if questions about copyright use ever arise.

- **Credit Creators When Required**: If a track's license specifies attribution, make sure you credit the creator properly. This is usually a simple mention in your podcast's show notes or at the end of the episode.

5. Avoiding Copyrighted Music

Using copyrighted music without permission can result in copyright strikes or legal issues. Even short clips of popular songs may violate copyright, so always opt for royalty-free, Creative Commons, or public domain tracks to ensure you're in the clear.

By sourcing royalty-free music and sound effects from trusted platforms and understanding licensing terms, you can enhance your podcast's soundscape legally and ethically. Using audio responsibly not only protects your podcast but also respects the work of other creators, contributing to a positive and creative community.

Podcasting Contracts

Contracts play a vital role in podcasting, whether you're collaborating with co-hosts, hosting guest speakers, or securing sponsorships. They establish clear expectations, protect your rights, and reduce the risk of misunderstandings or disputes. Here's why contracts are essential and some key clauses to include when drafting agreements for collaborations, guest appearances, and sponsorships.

1. Collaborations and Co-Hosting Agreements

If you're working with a co-host or collaborator, a contract helps outline each person's role, responsibilities, and rights. This agreement clarifies everything from content creation to profit-sharing, helping prevent conflicts down the road. Essential clauses to include are:

- **Roles and Responsibilities**: Define each person's role, such as who handles editing, social media, or episode planning. This ensures everyone knows what's expected of them.

- **Revenue Sharing**: Specify how revenue (from ads, sponsorships, or merchandise) will be divided. This is especially important if you plan to monetize the podcast.

- **Intellectual Property**: Clearly state who owns the podcast's content and branding. Will both parties have equal rights to the content, or will one person retain ownership?

- **Exit Strategy**: Outline what happens if one person wants to leave the podcast. This includes transferring ownership or the possibility of buying out the other person's share.

A detailed co-hosting agreement can prevent misunderstandings, especially as your podcast grows and generates revenue.

2. Guest Appearance Agreements

Guest contracts are a good practice for protecting both your podcast and your guest's interests. A guest appearance contract ensures that everyone agrees on how the recorded content can be used and shared. Key clauses to consider include:

- **Usage Rights**: Specify how you can use the recording, such as distributing it on podcast platforms, using it for promotional clips, or repurposing it in future content. Make sure the guest understands and agrees to this usage.

- **Promotion**: If you expect your guest to promote their appearance on their own platforms, include a promotion clause that outlines what's expected. This is optional but can help boost the reach of your episode.

- **Release and Waiver**: Include a release clause that waives the guest's rights to the recorded material. This gives you full control over the content without any future claims from the guest.

- **Compensation (if applicable)**: If you're offering any form of payment or incentive for guest appearances, specify the amount and payment terms. Most guest appearances are unpaid, but if compensation is offered, it's best to clarify the details.

A guest appearance agreement protects your podcast from legal claims while ensuring both parties are clear about expectations and usage.

3. Sponsorship Agreements

Sponsorship contracts are essential for formalizing the terms of an advertising partnership. They outline the sponsor's obligations, what they're paying for, and the content and timing of ads. Essential clauses include:

- **Payment Terms**: Clearly define the payment amount, payment method, and due date. Many sponsorship deals work on a CPM (cost per thousand) basis, so clarify how payment will be calculated based on downloads or impressions.

- **Ad Deliverables**: Specify the ad type (e.g., pre-roll, mid-roll, or post-roll), the length of the ad, and the number of episodes in which it will appear. Include any requirements from the sponsor, such as specific talking points or approved language.

- **Exclusivity and Competitors**: Some sponsors may request exclusivity, meaning you can't promote competing products during the sponsorship term. If you agree to exclusivity, set clear boundaries to avoid conflicts.

- **Termination Clause**: Define under what circumstances the contract can be terminated, such as breach of terms or non-payment. This allows either party to exit the agreement if issues arise.

- **Content Control**: Retain control over how the ad is delivered. Sponsors may have guidelines, but as the host, you'll want the final say on ad placement and tone to keep it aligned with your show's brand.

A sponsorship agreement protects your podcast financially and ensures you and your sponsor are aligned on terms and expectations.

Tips for Securing Agreements

When approaching collaborations, guest appearances, or sponsorships, having a written contract ready demonstrates professionalism. Here are some practical tips:

- **Use Clear, Simple Language**: Make contracts easy to understand. Avoid excessive legal jargon so all parties feel comfortable with the terms.

- **Use Templates When Starting Out**: There are many legal template services available, like Rocket Lawyer or LegalZoom, which offer customizable templates for podcast agreements. They're a good starting point if you're new to contract drafting.

- **Be Open to Negotiation**: Contracts may need to be adjusted based on the other party's needs or requests. Being flexible and willing to negotiate helps secure agreements and strengthens relationships.

- **Get It in Writing**: Verbal agreements may seem sufficient, but written contracts provide clarity and a legal foundation if issues arise. Email is a simple way to confirm agreements in writing, even for smaller collaborations.

Contracts establish a framework that benefits both you and the people you work with, ensuring everyone is clear on their roles, rights, and obligations. With well-drafted agreements, you'll build strong, professional relationships while protecting your podcast's interests as it grows.

Alex Reid

Chapter 12

Analytics and Continuous Improvement

Tracking Listener Data

Understanding your audience is key to improving your podcast, and tracking listener data provides valuable insights into who your listeners are, what they enjoy, and how they engage with your content. Analytics tools can help you gather data on downloads, demographics, and listening patterns, allowing you to make data-driven decisions to enhance your show.

Most podcast hosting platforms, like Podbean, Libsyn, and Anchor, provide built-in analytics that track core metrics. Downloads are one of the primary metrics to monitor, as they indicate how many people are consuming your episodes. Reviewing download patterns over time helps you see if your audience is growing and identify which episodes resonate most. Peaks in downloads often suggest popular topics, while dips may signal content areas that need adjustment.

Demographics data is another valuable insight offered by most analytics tools, showing details like your listeners' age, gender, and geographic location. This information helps you tailor your content to your audience's preferences and even strategize for potential sponsors who want to reach that demographic. For example, if a large portion of your listeners are from a specific region, you can incorporate culturally relevant topics or references that make the show more relatable.

Listening patterns, such as how long listeners stay engaged and at which points they drop off, give you an idea of how captivating your episodes are. Tools like Spotify for Podcasters offer these engagement metrics, which can be helpful for refining episode structure and pacing. If you notice that listeners consistently tune out at a certain point, consider adjusting the episode length or experimenting with new formats to maintain their interest.

By regularly reviewing and interpreting this data, you can make informed decisions about your content, format, and promotion strategies. Analytics empower you to continuously improve your podcast by aligning it more closely with your audience's preferences, leading to a stronger, more engaged listener base.

Evaluating Episode Performance

Understanding which episodes resonate most with your audience can be the secret to crafting a truly engaging podcast. Analyzing the performance of individual episodes isn't just about numbers—it's about discovering what excites your listeners, what keeps them coming back, and how you can create more content they'll love. Here's how to dive into your episode metrics and uncover valuable insights while keeping it enjoyable and easy.

First, take a look at **download numbers**. Think of downloads as a pulse check on your podcast; they show how many people were intrigued enough to hit play. High download numbers indicate popular topics or well-promoted episodes, while lower numbers might suggest that the topic didn't hit the mark with your audience or could benefit from a different angle next time. Keep an eye on any episodes that see a sudden spike in downloads—those can signal a topic or format that struck a chord.

Next, explore **listener retention** metrics, especially if you're using platforms like Spotify or Apple Podcasts, which provide detailed engagement stats. Retention rates show how long listeners stay tuned in. Did a significant portion drop off halfway through? Maybe the intro was too long, or there was a lull in the pacing. Alternatively, if retention is strong all the way through, you're onto something. A compelling story, well-paced content, or an exciting guest can all contribute to strong listener retention. Use this data to identify patterns—knowing where listeners typically tune out can be a goldmine for refining episode structure and content flow.

Another powerful metric is **listener feedback and ratings**. Ratings, reviews, and comments are direct feedback from your listeners, giving you a clearer sense of what they're enjoying (or not). Reviews often reveal deeper insights that numbers alone can't provide. Are listeners frequently mentioning a particular guest they loved? Did they find a specific topic especially insightful or funny? These comments can guide your future episode planning. Don't forget to look at social media interactions too; posts about new episodes can show you what listeners are sharing and talking about, pointing to topics that spark conversation.

Lastly, consider the **growth over time** of each episode. Some episodes might start slow but gain traction as they're shared, especially if the content is evergreen. By looking at how an episode performs weeks or even months after release, you can identify which topics have staying power—those are the ones that continue to attract new listeners and have lasting relevance.

By paying attention to downloads, retention, feedback, and long-term growth, you'll start to see patterns that tell you more about your audience's tastes and preferences. Evaluating episode performance isn't just about data; it's a way to get closer to your audience, crafting content that not only reaches them but resonates deeply. And with each insight, you're equipped to build a podcast that keeps listeners excited for what's next.

Strategies for Growth and Improvement

Building a successful podcast is a journey, and continuous growth comes from refining your content, exploring fresh ideas, and connecting with your audience in new ways. Here's a roadmap for growing your podcast and keeping it dynamic, engaging, and ever-evolving.

1. Refine Content with Listener Feedback

Your listeners are your best resource for improvement. Pay close attention to feedback through reviews, social media, and any direct messages or emails you receive. Look for recurring comments—are listeners loving your interviews but finding solo episodes too long? Maybe they're asking for more deep dives on certain topics. Use this feedback to fine-tune your episode format, pacing, or content choices. Consider creating a survey for listeners to gather more structured feedback, asking what they'd like to see more of, what could improve, and any new topics they're interested in. Listening closely and responding to feedback not only improves your content but shows your audience that their opinions matter.

2. Experiment with New Formats and Episode Structures

Keeping your podcast fresh is key to retaining and growing your audience. If you usually do solo episodes, try adding guest interviews or panel discussions. Or, if your episodes are typically long, experiment with short, "mini" episodes that focus on a single question or concept. You could even try storytelling or narrative episodes if your content allows. Testing new formats keeps your podcast from feeling repetitive and may help you discover a style that resonates even more with your listeners. Monitor listener engagement and feedback on these new episodes to see what works best, and don't be afraid to mix it up.

3. Explore Cross-Promotion and Collaboration

Collaborating with other podcasters or influencers in your niche is a powerful way to grow your audience. Reach out to similar podcasts for guest appearances, where you can tap into each other's listener bases. Cross-promotion on social media can also introduce your podcast to new followers, while interviews with other podcasters bring fresh perspectives to your show. Collaboration not only broadens your reach but also builds connections within the podcasting community, adding credibility and variety to your content.

4. Enhance Your Marketing Strategy

An effective marketing strategy can amplify your podcast's reach and attract new listeners. Start by identifying where your audience spends the most time—whether that's Instagram, Twitter, LinkedIn, or niche forums. Share engaging snippets, quotes, and highlights from your episodes to create excitement. Consistency is key, so set a social media calendar and post regularly. Experiment with different content types, like video teasers, Q&A sessions, or behind-the-scenes content, to see what resonates most. Email marketing is another valuable tool: create a newsletter with episode updates, bonus content, or early access to upcoming shows to build a stronger connection with your subscribers.

5. Invest in Audio Quality and Production Value

As your podcast grows, consider upgrading your equipment or enhancing your editing process to improve audio quality. Clearer sound and smoother editing elevate your content's professional appeal, helping you retain and attract new listeners. You don't have to invest in a full studio setup, but a high-quality microphone, good editing software, and perhaps some acoustic treatment can go a long way. Better production makes each episode more enjoyable to listen to, which can lead to more word-of-mouth recommendations and positive reviews.

6. Monitor Analytics and Set Growth Goals

Regularly tracking your analytics allows you to see what's working and what needs improvement. Keep an eye on metrics like downloads, retention, and listener demographics. Look for episodes that performed exceptionally well, then analyze what made them successful—was it the topic, guest, or timing? Use this data to set achievable growth goals, like increasing monthly downloads by 20% or expanding your listener base in a specific region. Setting concrete goals keeps you motivated and provides a clear focus for improvement.

7. Re-evaluate and Adjust Based on Trends

Podcasting trends are always evolving, so stay updated on new developments in the industry. Whether it's the rise of shorter episodes, video podcasts, or popular topics in your niche, being adaptable keeps your content relevant. Occasionally, reassess your branding and topic choices to ensure they align with audience interests and trends. Experiment with new approaches while staying true to your podcast's core identity.

By following these steps and continuously experimenting, adapting, and refining your approach, you'll build a podcast that grows organically, stays fresh, and keeps your audience engaged. Growth and improvement aren't about changing everything at once; they're about making small, strategic adjustments that add up over time, making your podcast stronger and more compelling with each episode

Conclusion

Congratulations on reaching the end of this guide! By now, you've gained the knowledge and tools to create, grow, and monetize a successful podcast. Podcasting is an incredible journey that lets you share your voice, connect with others, and make a meaningful impact. As you move forward, remember that the most successful podcasters aren't necessarily those with the fanciest equipment or the biggest budgets—they're the ones who stay committed, keep improving, and consistently deliver content that resonates with their audience.

This book was designed to be a roadmap you can return to at any stage of your podcasting journey. Whether you're refining your brand, planning new content, or exploring ways to engage with listeners, feel free to revisit the chapters that offer the guidance you need. As your podcast evolves, keep experimenting, learning from your listeners, and, most importantly, enjoying the creative process.

If you found value in this book, consider sharing your thoughts by leaving a review on Amazon. Your feedback not only helps other aspiring podcasters discover this resource but also supports the creation of more helpful content for the podcasting community. Thank you for allowing this book to be a part of your podcasting journey—I'm excited to see where it takes you.

Happy podcasting!

Alex Reid

Alex Reid

Alex Reid